Let Joy Be Your JOURNEY

Barbara Pedersen

Let Joy Be Your Journey

© 2021 Barbara Pedersen

Photographic images used in the lessons Copyright 2021 Rinkey Boleman

Paperback ISBN: 978-1-66780-982-3
eBook ISBN: 978-1-66780-983-0

With God's grace I have lived in joy most of my life. These lessons come from my perception of what can help anyone find joy. In addition to teaching joy to thousands of educators all over the world, I credit my learning to the students I have been blessed to teach and God's plan for my life.

This book is dedicated to my three sons, Jeff, Doug, and Todd, who have taught me more about faith, life, and love, than they ever learned from me. May their lives always be filled with the same joy they have given me.

My eternal gratitude will always be to God, who makes joy possible, and my late husband, Tom, who taught me more than I realized.

Let the journey begin.........

"The Joy of the Lord is Your Strength."
Nehemiah 8:10

To My Grandchildren

The lessons in this book are written for you, my dear grandchildren, Jack, Hannah, Charlie, George, Matt, Lydia, Tommy, Lauren, and Nick. You have brought me joy and reminded me about the meaning of life. You have validated my belief in the power of imagination and creativity. You are unique and blessed. Each one of you came into this world with special gifts from God. I can only imagine where your paths in life will take you and all the amazing adventures and blessings that lie ahead for each of you. My hope is that these lessons will help you find joy on your journey called life. Now may God continue to guide you and help you find your purpose.

"Life is not measured by the number of breaths we take,
but by the moments that take our breath away."
Maya Angelou

CONTENTS

LESSON ONE

<u>Perspective</u>

"It's not what you look at that matters; it is what you see."
Henry David Thoreau

Perspective About Life

Your perspective depends on what you believe, based on your life experiences and the influences of the people who come into your life. On the other hand, we never know how others are interpreting life. Somebody could have the same experience as someone else but have created a completely different meaning from it. Because of that, remember that your hope is to find joy; you need to pay attention to how you are thinking about people, events, situations, and places. Instead of judging the perspective of others, stay focused on your own perception about life.

When it comes down to the truth about you, other people's perspectives may or may not be right, so you must live your life based on what you believe to be true, not based on of what others may think about you. Walk your talk, talk your walk, and have outstanding principles in life that are worthy for you to live up to.

"The only thing you sometimes have control
over is perspective. You don't have control over your situation.
But you have a choice how you view it."
Chris Pine

Same Experiences: Different Perspectives

I was at the airport one day, and a little boy was running beside me in front of his parents. I said to him, "Isn't the airport amazing? How fun to see all of these airplanes." He looked at me and said, "Oh no, there is the best part of the airport, McDonald's." Even with a multitude of planes, his excitement was all about McDonald's.

His comments help to illustrate why the more experiences you have in life, the more ideas you have about what you understand. He had found joy seeing McDonald's inside another building and the fact that it was familiar. It seems the planes would have brought him more joy, but that wasn't his perspective. In your life, you may go to the airport and your only joy is getting through security. Others find joy in different ways, even though they are having the same experiences.

When looking for joy, how you look at life makes a difference. Many analogies exist for this idea such as, "Is your glass half full or is it half empty?" "When you have lemons, can you make lemonade or is life sour?" Life experiences can have a positive twist or a negative one, depending on your perspective. I love the story of the two workers hauling heavy stones in a wheelbarrow. When asked what they were doing, the first replied, "Hauling rocks," and the second replied, "I'm building a cathedral." How do you see what you are doing right now? Are you finding joy? Do you need to change your perception?

Remember, how you respond is all about your own perspective. No matter what the situation is, you may see the same thing that I see, but that doesn't mean you and I will have the same perspective. We may see things differently, and that is all right.

> *"Return to my woods and see it in a different way.*
> *Perhaps the trees have a new story."*
> Henry David Thoreau

Different Experiences: Same Perspective

Sometimes we can have different situations that lead to the same perspective. As I walked through the house one day, Lydia, my grand-daughter, was reading *Call of the Wild* by Jack London; Hannah, another granddaughter, was watching the movie "Jaws", and my dog Bear was watching squirrels playing in the back yard. "Survival" was the idea that connected all these experiences but through different eyes. Author, Jack London, believed that you needed to live your lives and not just exist. His perspective of survival was quite different from a squirrel looking for a nut. But when you think about it, Jack London and the squirrel were both looking for a way to find joy in survival.

How Do You Change Your Perspective?

How you perceive people and events affects how you see your own life. One person's perspective about a situation may be completely different from someone else's. Different perceptions in any group or family can be very healthy in helping you understand and see new points of view. You may find a new belief when you take the time to listen to other people's perception about life.

Find out more than your first impression about people. Asking questions and paying attention to others will help you understand them. You may have an opinion about someone you know based on what that person may have said or done at one time. However, your opinion may be skewed, especially if you are basing it on a narrow perspective.

Before you have a final opinion about someone or an event, ask yourself:

1. Do I have all the facts?

If you are basing what you believe about someone or something by your first impression, you may not have enough information to draw an accurate conclusion. Ask questions.

2. Is my information from a reliable source?

When you are fact finding, consider your source. You can't believe everything online, in print, or from the media if the information isn't from a reliable source.

3. On what am I basing my perception?

If your viewpoint is just hearsay or your initial thought, then consider rethinking your perception until you have more information.

4. Was I too quick to come to my perception?

Your first conviction may turn out to be correct but be sure you have spent adequate time determining your point of view.

5. Is my perspective about people or situations helping me find joy?

Sometimes your opinion may actually upset you, make you mad, or bring you to a negative conclusion. Check your emotion to see if you are finding joy. If not, you may want to change your mind about your perspective and see if you can't find something, no matter how small, that is positive.

Life can sometimes make you annoyed or angry. Perhaps you can act on the issue to be an advocate to change something that isn't right. Your perception about life will be influenced by your ability to discover the truth and to find meaning in the world around you. The more you learn, the greater perspective you will have.

"Strong minds discuss ideas; average minds discuss events; weak minds discuss people."
Socrates

A Perspective that Changed

You appreciate what you know and understand, which creates your perspective about people and your surroundings. If you doubt that, let me give you an example of how perceptions can change. I was at the zoo, standing by the monkey cage watching all the monkeys jumping around, and a little boy ran up to the cage. I said to him, "Aren't the monkeys amazing?" I couldn't believe it when he said," Not the monkeys, look at the tire swing. I rode on a tire once, and it was so much fun." His comment illustrates how we all find joy in different ways. Will his perspective about the zoo change in time? That will be his choice based on his life experiences.

Perspectives can change. My view about zoos was positive as a child, but as an adult I became an advocate against zoos housing large animals in small habitats that do not resemble their natural environment. Thirty years ago, when I went to an eastern city to teach fifty students for a week while fifty teachers observed my strategies, I decided to take the students on a bus to visit a local city zoo to observe different animals and their behavior. To prepare the class, we watched live telecasts from the San Diego Zoo showing animals in large habitats designed to mimic their native homeland. In contrast, when we arrived at the city zoo, there were several animals in small concrete cages with no vegetation and one elephant shackled to a concrete floor with hardly room for her to turn around. I was appalled. Never had I experienced such animal abuse firsthand. After returning to the school, my first question was, "Did this zoo look anything like the live videos we saw before our study trip?" Then I asked if the students thought the elephant was living in an environment that resembled her natural habitat. The students replied, "No, it didn't look anything like where she should be living."

We immediately decided as a class that we would do a social action and try to get Toni, the elephant, moved to a better zoo. The students dived into research to find out that elephants lived in groups and walked long distances every day, but here was a young elephant living in solitary confinement. Elephants should never be kept without any peers, plus Toni had developed arthritis in the lower joint of her left leg because she was forced to stand in a concrete pen all day. Now the children were also appalled, and they were determined to save Toni, the elephant.

We invited city officials for our group presentations, and each student presented a reason Toni needed a better environment. Eventually, Toni was relocated to the National Zoo in Washington D.C. with acknowledgement that the local zoo had been unsuitable. There is nothing quite like a group of students or adults who realize their actions can make a difference in their world. If you believe that there needs to be a change made in your life from your perspective, just do it!

> *"Faith gives you an inner strength and a sense*
> *of balance and perspective in life."*
> Gregory Peck

Your Perspective Matters

How we interpret things in our lives, determines our personal joy and success.

   1.   Perspective of Ability

For example, you could be playing golf poorly, but you have a choice about how to look at that experience. You could decide you are not a good player, and you don't ever want to play again. You just aren't as skilled as you thought. Or you can decide that there are some skills you need to work on. Or you may need help from an expert. Your deciding factor is to ask yourself, "How much do I love golf?" Try choosing to follow your joy. Never give up something that you are passionate about. So, either give up and stop what you are doing, or get up and get better.

   2.   Perspective of Self

Some students that I taught thought they couldn't be successful, so my goal as a teacher was to help them change their perspective. Poor self-perception has stopped great builders, amazing architects, outstanding doctors, and inspiring teachers. If you see yourself inadequate to achieve something, you are probably going to live out your self-proclaimed prophecy. You need to know you have a choice in life about how you perceive your future.

> *"If you hear a voice within you say, 'You cannot paint.' By all means,*
> *paint and that voice will be silenced."*
> Vincent Van Gogh

3. Your Perspective Can Be a Misconception

Speaking of school, at my class reunion an interesting incident happened about perspective. One person had carried a misconception of another student through the years and had just found out that what she had perceived was not true. Joy finding is an ongoing process. You can't keep yourself locked in a misconception. Be a truth seeker. Anytime you feel negative about something or someone, seek the truth and move on. Don't be a prisoner in your own misconception.

> *"Try to see things differently. It's the only way to get a*
> *clear perspective on the world and on your life."*
> Neal Shusterman

Are You "Making It"?

I would be amiss if I didn't comment on the perception of "making it" in life. Some might think you "make it" when you have a degree or wealth. But I believe that "making it" in life is finding out that your passion plus perseverance is bringing you joy.

I have seen many students "make it" over the years. One of my favorite students was Steve. He had a lot of personal issues but worked hard and achieved success in school and in creating relationships. Years later a sanitation truck was coming down the street where I had parked at an elementary school. I waved. A young man jumped off the truck and stopped me. I didn't recognize him at first, but when he said who he was, we hugged in the middle of the street. There was Steve, all grown up, married with two children, and working for the sanitation department. He said to me, "I wanted you to know that you always said I would make it, and I have. Thank you, Mrs. Pedersen." Thank you, Steve, for choosing to find your joy.

I learned that day that "making it" could mean many things. If you have a roof over your head, food on your table, people you love in your life, and joy with what you are doing, you have made it. You can make it too. Just believe.

Your Perspective About Others

Look and look again. When you take time to find out more than your first impression, you begin to find out who someone really is. Perhaps you can remember being on a team or in a class at school when you may have made a judgment about someone there without really knowing too much about that person. Your first perception may now be different because experiences and time can change what you think. Don't judge too quickly before really knowing the full story.

"When you wake up every day, you have two choices.
You can either be positive or negative; an optimist or a pessimist.
I choose to be an optimist. It is all a matter of perspective."
Harvey Mackay

Even Dogs Have a Perspective About Life

Dogs are good teachers about feelings. I never met a dog that carried a grudge. Dogs get over things, and move right on to the next experience, and life is good. When I think about dogs I have had, I don't remember any that were not happy most of the time. They may have been sad when

I walked out the door, but when I came back their tails were wagging, and they were excited to see me even if I had only been gone ten minutes. They could have moped around annoyed that I had been gone so long, but that never happened. As soon as the door opened, they were excited to see me with smiles on their faces. I like to think my dogs genuinely love me, but the truth may be that they don't understand time, or they always keep a positive perspective on life.

My collie Bentley passed away. He had been very close at the time to my youngest dog, Bear. Bear was devastated and laid by Bentley's bed for a long time. In time, he seemed to accept it and moved on with his life. Occasionally, Bear would lay in Bentley's favorite spot, which made me think it was his way of remembering good times. I would say to him, "Bentley was a good friend, wasn't he?" He would always look up and seem to smile. Bear is now the big brother to a golden retriever named Murphy. Perhaps Murphy will have special memories about Bear.

Dogs are great teachers and certainly know how to love. The dogs in my life have made me a better person. If you are a dog person, you probably have the same perspective.

"Yesterday I was a dog. Tomorrow, I'll probably still be a dog.
Sigh! There's so little hope for advancement."
Charles M. Schultz

Final Word

Your perspective plays into every experience you have in life. You not only will make meaning of what is going on today from your past experiences, but you will also create meaning from what you believe to be true. A close cousin to perspective is judgment. One of the most important lessons I have learned in my life is not to be too quick to judge someone else.

When judgment comes into my mind, I immediately ask myself if it is true or just someone's opinion. Seek to understand; it is common for us to judge countries, events, people, and situations. You may not like a political leader or a person's point of view, but if you seek to understand something or someone, your feelings can improve. You don't need to change your point of view, but if you listen, you can understand why people's lives and experiences cause them to think differently than you do about the same thing.

Spending too much time being judgmental separates you from others. If we take the time to understand others, we discover different viewpoints and we grow in our thinking. Sometimes it seems that people are put in our path to teach us important life lessons about perspective.

Affirmations for Perspective

- Today I will choose to see things from an optimistic perspective.
- Today I will see my own life in a new and exciting way.
- Today I will find good in every circumstance.
- Today I will try to see my life as God sees it.
- Today I will make my own sunshine, no matter what the weather is.

LESSON TWO

<u>Change</u>

"What the caterpillar calls the end of the world,
the Master calls a butterfly."
Richard Bach

Change Brings Joy

Change was chosen for the joy journey because if you cannot change the circumstances that need to be different in your life, then joy will be hard to find. Many lessons in our lives show us that change is a good thing and happens often. A tree turns colors every season, a tadpole becomes a frog, you evolve as you grow older, and all of us change our minds on occasion.

Some situations can't be changed. However, if circumstances need to be otherwise and it is possible, just do it because positive changes bring us joy. Changes are a way of God leading you to where you need to be. Because of free will, sometimes a decision doesn't turn out well and that is a clue that you need to reconsider and move on again. This lesson about change in our lives will lead into the next lesson about choice. Choice and change are cousins. You might have a choice, if you are going to make a change, but not always.

"God, grant me the serenity to accept the things I cannot change, courage to change the things I can, and wisdom to know the difference."
Reinhold Niebuhr

Life Changing

My favorite story about change happened when I met a boy named Darius, a seventh-grade student. As an educational consultant, I often would teach at middle schools to demonstrate new best teaching practices. In preparation for these events, I would visit the middle school classroom I would be teaching in to gain an understanding of the environment, social interactions and the curriculum they were studying. Unfortunately, this particular classroom was completely out of control. The teacher taught like everyone was listening, but no one was paying attention. Most of the students were talking or walking around the room; however, the teacher went right on teaching. Learning wasn't happening. I knew this classroom of students would be challenge.

The next day I greeted the students at the door and had their chairs arranged in a circle. I told them to sit anywhere because I wanted to get to know them. We went around the circle and said who we were, then I asked them, "When was the last time you read a book?" The majority agreed that it was third grade. I told them we were going to the library where I wanted them to go to the young children's section and pick out a book they remembered reading or that was read to them.

As we walked across campus back to our room, there was an air of excitement about the books they found. Darius was walking next to me, and he had the book, *Green Eggs and Ham* by Dr. Seuss. I told him that I remembered my children loving that book. Anytime my sons didn't want to try to taste something new, I always reminded them about *Green Eggs and Ham*. He asked me what book I found, and I had chosen *Curious George*. I told him I still loved *Curious George* and still watched cartoons about him.

When we returned to class, we shared our books and how we felt when we thought about reading them again. It was a start in changing the climate in the classroom, but only a start. We discussed in our circle how to make changes in our lives.

The next day I introduced the Life Goals: Do the Right Thing and Treat People Right, even if you don't feel like it. These two short goals have a big message to help anyone make positive changes in their life. I will go into more depth in another lesson.

Then the class continued the discussion about using the Life Goals daily. We started with five ways we could make a difference in our lives using the Life Goals:

1. Start small when making changes, like holding the door for someone or helping pick up papers dropped at a locker. Once you realize that small changes aren't that difficult to make, you can start making bigger changes in your life.

2. Do what is right when no one is watching.

3. Do what is right without a reward.

4. You may need to change friends to do what is right.

5. When treating people right doesn't seem fair, try to change your mind. Treating people right will keep you out of trouble, but most importantly, it is the right thing to do. Go Life Goals!

As I was walking across the courtyard on my last day at that school, I saw Darius picking up a paper and throwing it in a trash can. I walked over and thanked him. He said, "Didn't you say that we need to start with the small things that needed to change, and then we can build up to changing big things in our life?" I fought back the tears and realized how special Darius really was. I prayed he would have the strength to make the changes he needed to make in his life. Picking up paper was a beginning; now he could start working on changing bigger things.

> *"Practice yourself, for heaven's sake in little things,*
> *and then proceed to greater."*
> Epictetus

I learned a great lesson from Darius. We all have the opportunity to encourage each other in reaching one's potential, but you are the one who must make the decision to change for the better.

> *"It is not the strongest of the species that survive,*
> *nor the most intelligent, but the one most responsive to change."*
> Charles Darwin

Pay Attention to What You Want to Change

When you pay attention, you know what you want to change.

1. What are you doing?

   Do your actions need to be changed? When you pay attention to what you are doing, you may find that your life is becoming unmanageable. If so, it is time to make some changes.

   a. If you are making negative choices, deciding to change is the first step.

   b. Realizing what kind of actions need to replace your present actions is the second step.

   c. Implementing the positive actions to replace the negative choices is the third step. You should then notice that your life is becoming more manageable.

You can change a bad habit by keeping track of when you are doing it. Try to mark down how many times you do what you are trying to change. While you are conscious of what you want to do differently, you can make that change. Remember that changing a habit takes effort and determination. Change usually isn't an easy fix; it takes perseverance. When you believe it, you will achieve it!

2. What are you thinking?

   What you think about can become your truth if you believe it. Pay attention to what is on your mind. Are your thoughts true, bringing you joy or putting you in a bad mood? Thinking affects our actions. Watch your thinking and it will stop you from doing something you don't want to do. Change can happen in many ways. You may believe you need to start working out, reading more, drinking more water, or making another positive change that will improve your health or life. Change can also involve situations that you wish were different with other people. Sometimes students run with the wrong crowd. In that case, everyone in the group probably needs to change, but remember, you can only change yourself. You can't change others unless they want to change.

"The world we have created is a product of our thinking; it
cannot be changed without changing our thinking."
Albert Einstein

3. How are you feeling?

Emotion drives attention. Thinking and actions are driven by how you feel. What feelings do you have right now? Could they lead to a negative action? Is it time to change emotions? Just as the seasons change, you also change every year. As you grow, you may learn things about yourself that you want to change such as learning something new or improving a skill. As good as you are, you can always get better, but that may take making a change and using effort.

"I can't change the direction of the wind, but I can
adjust my sails to always reach my destination."
Jimmy Dean

When Do You Need to Change What You Are Thinking?

If you have negative thinking, sometimes you just need to change your mind.

Here are four tips for changing your mind:

1. Don't dread doing anything. Just change your mind about what is bothering you. I used to dread going to the doctor or dentist, but now I accept it and expect the best. Is there something you dread doing? Is there someone you dread seeing? Change your mind. Decide you are not going to dread it, and instead start looking forward to it. Make up your mind that you will enjoy it if you give yourself a chance. Most of the time things you dread turn out to be fun.

2. Don't worry. Worry is a waste of time. Worrying about things that haven't happened yet makes no sense. Maybe they will never happen, but if they do, you can face them then. I always figure I need to postpone my worrying and just plan to fall apart if something bad actually happens.

3. Regret can be a real joy stealer. Don't regret something you did or said for the rest of your life. You can make amends to the person you hurt or offended. If you really didn't do anything wrong, or you didn't get to do something you wanted to do, get over it and quit carrying regret with you. Regretting something isn't going to make it better, and time is wasted in regret when there is nothing you can do to change it. It is over and that is ok. If I texted something I wish I hadn't, instead of spending time regretting it, I make amends and move on.

4. Change the words in your head. Watch your self-talk so you don't say things like, "I'm fat. I'm stupid. I don't deserve this." As you envision, so it will be. Years ago, if you wanted to be thinner, you put a picture of your thinner self on the

refrigerator door, keeping the positive image you wanted in front of you. When you practice positive self-talk and use images, you are protected from negative thoughts. I used to take pictures of students doing the right thing. If a student had trouble listening, I would show him a picture of himself being a good listener. It helped to tell him, "You were a great listener in this picture. I know you can listen like that again."

5.   When you wake up, think to yourself that today is going to be a great day. Remember to appreciate that you have another day to enjoy what is around you. Why not celebrate everything? Today I got new tires on my car. I know, amazing right? I was so excited, and they looked wonderful. There was a time when hearing that I needed new tires would have been bad news. When the car guy came to get me from the waiting room to tell me my car was ready, I looked at my car and said loudly, "These tires look amazing. They are so black and shiny. Thank you so much because there is nothing like new tires. I'm so happy, I'm glad I decided to change them all." He told me I was the first person he ever saw who was that excited about new tires.

The words in your head can influence you and changing your thoughts does require self-control. You must want to control your thinking and be selective about what you put in your mind. Remember the saying, "Garbage in, garbage out." The more positive the things you watch or read, the more positive the effects will be in your brain. So, when you are not getting positive results, pay attention to what's on your mind. You may need to change your thinking to something positive. Look out the window and appreciate nature. That is always positive.

"You are where your thoughts have brought you.
You will be tomorrow where your thoughts take you."
Ralph Waldo Emerson

Change the Story

For years I traveled across the United States consulting with different school districts about how to treat people right and do the right thing. On a typical day, I would work with school-wide staff members on how to build relationships with their students using strategies to develop trust among the school community for authentic learning to happen. I would drive away from the school feeling excited and empowered by the changes happening, only to find my joy beginning to vanish because of the 2002 red Dodge Charger veering down the turn lane trying to cut into my lane. It was the same lane I had patiently been waiting in for the last 45 minutes to go all of 100 yards. My diminishing joy turned me into a crazy person that I didn't know or recognize. I found myself talking to the other drivers, "Don't let him in, and tighten up. He is a line cutter. He used to cut in grade school, high school, and he is still cutting. It's time he learns a lesson. Don't let him in."

How could I go from a happy person to this kind of behavior? One day, it hit me. These line cutters were stealing my joy, and they didn't even know it. How could I waste this much energy over such petty behavior? The question became what do I do when I start feeling that way? I began to change the story!

No one really knows what the story is, so why not make it positive? For all we know, the guy in the Dodge Charger received a call that his dad was in the hospital, or maybe he had severe diarrhea and was trying to make it to the nearest restroom. Make the story work for you. You will find life is less stressful, and you will have more joy when you change the story.

Final Word

If you really want to change something, you have the power to do so. Sometimes change takes courage and change that lasts always takes time. Be courageous and make change happen for you and others.

Changes in nature do not happen fast if they are to last. The fast changes are usually destructive like a tornado or an earthquake, while the development of the seasons and the metamorphosis of the cocoon to the butterfly take time. All the things in nature show us we can make changes in our own lives. You never stop changing and growing. You will learn new ideas and then decide what you want to do in your life so you can develop the skills you will need to make your dreams happen.

Never be afraid of change; just embrace it. It will take you to where you are supposed to be. When changes happen that you didn't choose, remember that changes eventually work for good even when it doesn't seem that way at the time.

Remember changes have a way of making you a better person. Just believe that you can help make the world a better place by your actions. God has a plan for you, just like His plan for the cocoon. God believes in you and loves you no matter what you are going through.

"Progress is impossible without change; and those who cannot change their minds cannot change anything."
Bernard Shaw

Affirmations for Change

- I can make the changes that need to be made in my life with the help of God.

- I will trust that my steps are being directed, and that any changes I need to make will come easily.

- I will accept the changes in my life that I cannot change.

LESSON THREE

<u>Choice</u>

"Two roads diverged in a wood, and I—I took the one less traveled by,
and that has made all the difference."

Robert Frost

Joy is a Choice

You might wonder how choice can bring you joy. The answer is that having options in life can make you happy, but what you do with your choices can bring you great joy.

Life is full of choices. Your actions and your attitude depend on what you do with your choice. Life gives us many opportunities to choose different paths to pursue. You will know when you are on the right path, because you will find your passion.

If you want to be happy right now, you may have to choose to change your mind about your past. It is time to work on today, not yesterday. That is your choice.

Starting this lesson about choice takes me to my oldest grandson who has chosen many paths to follow during his young life. He has always participated successfully in many sports growing up. Watching him play baseball in middle school and high school made you know he had found his passion.

However, when entering his junior year of high school, Jack announced that he was choosing to leave the baseball team. He wasn't going to pursue being a professional baseball player, and he decided to use his time for other things. He still loved baseball, but he made the choice that the game wasn't going to consume his life. He is now in college studying architecture and who knows, he may design a baseball stadium someday.

Would everyone make the same choice that Jack did? No, but the choices you make need to be from your heart talking to your head and what is right for you. You can't live your life depending on what other people choose. Your life is yours to create. You will not find joy if you are making choices to please other people.

*"Here at college, I literally choose my own life. I am in control of
what I am studying, who I am hanging out with,
what my faith looks like, and the life decisions that are right for me.
Life is about choices and finding the ones that bring you joy."*
Hannah Pedersen

When Others' Choices Matter

*"Too often in life, something happens, and you might blame
other people for not being happy. We all have choices,
and we make the choice to accept situations or not."*
Tom Brady

When Andrew Luck retired from the Indianapolis Colts, he said, "I haven't been able to live the life I want to live. It's taken the joy out of this game. The only way forward for me is to remove myself from football."

Andrew Luck left the field at Lucas Oil Stadium for the last time to a shower of boos from the Colt's fans, who had learned during the game that he was leaving football. As much as you may have loved Andrew Luck as a Colt, you should love him more for making a hard choice and wish him the best as he enters this new chapter of his life. I hope Andrew knows that many are cheering loudly about his decision. You want his choice to be right for him. You can't make choices for other people's lives, especially if you don't know the whole story.

*"I've learned that you have to make careful choices because
everything has an impact. I've also learned that you can't please
everyone in life, so please yourself and figure out what really matters."*
Gretchen Bieller

When the Choice You Make Doesn't Go Well

Every choice in life does not always work out the way you envisioned. When you decide one thing, but it doesn't go well, here are some points to remember:

1. When at first you don't succeed, try and try again.

2. Negative choices are not always bad. A lesson exists with every decision you make in life, good or bad. When decisions don't work out, look for the lesson. Learn from your choice.

3. You always have the option to have a positive attitude, no matter how poorly your choice turns out.

4. Following the Life Goals will help you make better choices. Do the right thing and treat people right.

5. When a choice goes poorly, it is not the end of the world. You can always make another choice.

"You may never know what results come of your action but if you do nothing, there will be no result."
Mahatma Gandhi

We Change as Our Choices Change

When you are young, your choices may not seem that big of a deal, but actually they are forming you into the person you are today. As a child you may be given the choice to eat macaroni and cheese or try something new like sushi. If you never try anything but macaroni and cheese, you may miss out on some great tastes in life. You may not be willing to try anything outside your comfort zone and it may even predict how much of a risk taker you will be.

As we grow up our decisions become more important. Will you drink alcohol at a party? Will you choose caring and responsible friends? Will you choose to do well in school? The options keep coming. What will you choose as a profession? Where do you want to live? Do you want to get married?

Each choice in life helps you to grow into a wiser person. Appreciate that your selections come with lessons, so don't miss the lessons given to you to learn and grow.

"Don't dwell on what went wrong. Instead, focus on what to do next. Spend your energies on moving forward toward finding the answer."
Denis Waitley

Take Your Choice

Since we are talking about choice, below you have four choices to work into your life. Choose one or all four, it's up to you.

1. Giving joy is better than getting joy.

2. Choose to be happy. Every morning get up and say, "Good morning God. Please direct my steps to follow your will. Help me make good decisions. Thanks."

3. Take Time To:

    Work; it is the price of success.

    Play; it is the secret of youth.

    Think; it is the source of power.

    Read; it is the fountain of wisdom.

    Pray; it is conversation with God.

    Laugh; it is music of the soul.

    Listen, it is the pathway to understanding.

    Dream; it is hitching your wagon to a star.

    Worship; it is the highway of reverence.

Love and be loved; it is the gift of God.

Author Unknown

4. Every morning chose to say this positive cheer, which I often say in the car.

I am happy.

I am healthy.

I am successful.

I am loving.

I am caring.

And every day in every way, I am getting better and better.

And believe it!!!

You have to believe it for it to happen.

"In the long run, we shape our lives, and we shape ourselves.
The process never ends until we die. And the choices we make
are ultimately our own responsibility."
Eleanor Roosevelt

Final Word

Life is all about choices. Should I do this or should I do that? You might find yourself asking, "Did I make the right choice?" Sometimes you don't know that answer until time passes, and you see the results of your choice.

Big choices take deliberation and a strong belief in your choice. Is your decision worth it? Could this decision end badly? How will you know if you are right? If you have an important choice to make, consider this advice.

1. Be sure you believe in the choice you make. When you believe something is right, you can move forward without looking back. Take responsibility for what you choose.

2. Talk about your decision with trusted friends or family. Sometimes getting another perspective on your choice can test, and prove, how strong your belief is about your decision.

3. The path you choose in life will bring you joy if you ask God to direct your steps. Pray for guidance.

4. Once you have made the decision about your choice, stick to it. Believe it enough that there is no turning back and move forward with focus and perseverance.

5. Not everyone has to believe what you believe, but if your choice will be a help to humanity and the world, go for it.

6. Take time for reflection on your choice along the way. You can always add, delete, or change as you pay attention to your results.

"You are the sum total of your choices."
Dr. Wayne Dyer

Affirmation for Choice
- I will choose what I think about.
- I will choose my words today.
- I will choose to have gratitude today.
- I will choose how I respond to things today.

LESSON FOUR

Patience

"We have always a resource in the skies.
They are constantly turning a new page to view."
Henry David Thoreau

Remembering Patience

Growing up seems to be full of opportunities to be patient. You have to wait your turn at the drinking fountain, for the school bus, and to see what grade you received on a test. As time passes, patience seems to involve bigger challenges. You wait to see if you were accepted into the college you wanted to attend or if you got a job you applied for. You realize that being patient while you wait for an event seems to be a part of life.

Patience is Not Just Waiting

I used to tell students that the important thing about learning patience is not waiting, but rather how you wait. Doing the right thing while waiting doesn't include pushing or arguing. Every once in a while, I would hear, "You stepped out of line, go to the back." then anger really grew. Today, those students now possibly are the ones who never let anyone get in front of them in traffic.

When I was teaching fourth grade, my colleague and I tried to involve the students in setting procedures for behavior. For example, there was always a problem when the children had to wait in a line. We had the students begin to problem solve and figure out how we could eliminate lines all the time. The class came up with the idea that when the whistle blew at the end of recess, they could quietly enter the building and walk to their classrooms. My colleague and I thought there was no way that was going to work. Surprisingly, when we tested it, students calmly entered the school from the playground, and walked straight to class. As a result, the fourth-grade classrooms never went back to recess lines. Their idea was a time saver, and the students were trusted that it would work. Students sometimes have better solutions than their teachers, if we teach problem solving, and trust them to do the right thing. Eliminating those lines improved everyone's behavior.

Patience Teaches Us Lessons

If it is hard for you to wait, then you can count on being handed repeated lessons about patience, which occur when we wait without judging events around us. You should not only accept the opportunity to wait, but also embrace it, learning the lesson patience teaches us.

I can remember some of my grandchildren waiting to see if they made the team they wanted, if they won the Science Fair, for a test result, or waiting to see what choir they made. If they never learned to wait on people, things, and time, they could have lost their joy. Remember to be joyful while you are waiting for something.

Patience is not just simply waiting. It is waiting with the anticipation of life handing you joyful experiences and lessons to learn. Don't wait for joy. You have it in you all the time. Just be patient and accept joy as it comes.

During a wait time try to realize how lucky you are to get to have that experience at all. The anticipation and hope that comes with waiting can remind you that what brought you to that moment was important. If waiting doesn't give you the results you wanted, remember every cloud has a silver lining. Now is the time for you to assess what you wanted to happen and if needed, improve on the skills you need or change your direction of where you are going.

Lack of Patience Can Be a Joy Stealer

I remember when one of my grandsons didn't make a basketball team he wanted to make. I never saw him discouraged. He joined another team, and even though it wasn't the team he wanted, he learned, practiced and excelled.

The next year he made the school team of his choice. If he had given up or decided not to play because it wasn't the team he wanted the first time, he might have missed a very important time in his life. Someday you may not get the college or job you wanted first, but remember, when you practice patience with a good attitude and keep giving all the effort you can, a better job or college experience will be around the corner.

Even if you didn't make the team, at least you tried out and were good enough to be considered. Not making something doesn't mean you are finished; it just means not yet. Changing direction or trying to use another one of your strengths could be an option.

Patience at the Grocery

There came a time in my life, where I made a conscious effort to work on improving my patience. I can tell you that, without a doubt, there is no better place to practice patience than the grocery store. I always hated going to the grocery. I still do. You park the car, walk a mile to the entrance only to grab a cart that inevitably has a sticky handle from God only knows what, an empty Starbucks cup rolling in the cart basket, and a bad wheel that will continue to annoy you throughout the grocery experience.

Now I must tell you, before I used patience, I had a bad habit of going to the grocery when I was hungry. My cart would be nearly full of items by the second isle. At this point, it would usually occur to me that I really didn't need the mega-bag of Cheetos. Instead of using the Life Goals and the Lifeline of patience to take the chip bag back to its proper place, I would carefully place it next to wherever it would fit at my current location, like next to the detergent or the frozen peas. Needless to say, a lot of cereal and cookies didn't make it back to the right place. Now, after working on patience, I always put items that I don't want back where they belong. I laughed yesterday when I saw a watermelon on the pasta shelf. It reminded me of old times. That must have been a shopper in training.

After what seems like eternity weaving up and down the isles to the point where you tell yourself, "It is time to get out of here," you are left with one of the biggest tests of patience, the dreaded checkout grocery line. Is there anything worse? It used to be so bad that sometimes I would get the people around me mad about waiting too. There would be a long line with only two cashiers, and one of them would be training someone to be a new clerk. I would act disgusted and suggest they train in the middle of the night. Before long, I would have the whole group of people in line complaining until the manger would come out and open a new line. Fast forward. Now that I use patience, I actually look forward to a long line to just relax and look at all the weird magazines by the check out.

Then of course there was the chore of returning the grocery cart after unloading the groceries into your car. I used to think I didn't have the time nor patience to return my cart after shopping. I would strategically place my cart next to the light pole and be on my way. Ironically, during my quest to improve my patience skills, I heard author Joyce Meyer talking about her use of patience and returning her grocery cart to the store. Her message was a meant to be. Now, no matter what the weather is, I walk the cart to where it belongs when I'm finished using it. Thank you, Joyce.

> *"Patience is not simply the ability to wait.*
> *It is how we behave while we're waiting."*
> Joyce Meyer

Patience Can Help Us Learn

When you become frustrated with the challenges in life and forget to be patient, you miss all the lessons that patience teaches. Educate yourself on skills to improve or practice a change in attitude while you have the opportunity to wait for something. The gift of time will bring clarity to your life.

Patience gives you the opportunity to learn what is important. When we don't understand someone's decision, be tolerant, be patient, because God will lead everyone in the right direction.

Remember to wait and to be patient when what you want doesn't happen immediately. Don't get discouraged when a storm hits. The storm will pass, and tomorrow will be a sunshiny day.

Waiting for the Wrong Bus

Patience was the key word in a fourth-grade study trip I took to the Indianapolis Motor Speedway, home of the Indianapolis 500 race. Growing up in Indianapolis, I had always gone to qualifications and the race, however, I had never been to Carburation Day. Out of the blue, a father of one of my students called and asked if I would like to bring my fourth-grade class to the speedway and meet the famous race car drivers Al Unser, Mario Andretti, and A.J. Foyt on, you guessed it, Carburation Day. I couldn't believe it!

We left the school at 7:00AM to meet our contact person at Gate 4. Much to my surprise when we arrived at the track, it looked like race day. The crowd was overwhelming. Now picture this; there were seventy fourth graders, two teachers, two parents and the bus driver on a big yellow bus. The police directed us to turn toward the track infield, however we soon realized that we were on the opposite side of where we needed to be. Traffic was horrible. We were now moving a snail's pace with people from all walks of life surrounding us. Unfortunately, we had to go by an area of the track called the snake pit. Back during these days, the snake pit was like Vegas, what happens at the snake pit, stays at the snake pit. I think some of the kids were traumatized by the events as I told them to "look away, look away." The good news was that because of the "being there" experience, I wouldn't have to teach inappropriate dress in public and that private body parts should always be covered. I also didn't need to teach the lesson "Say No to Drugs." We had great visuals of that lesson. I didn't even need to teach sex education, and lastly, I didn't need to discuss the problems of drinking underage.

I was standing next to the driver's seat and leaned over to Mr. Nicely, the bus driver and said, "We have to leave. We cannot let these kids get off the bus. We will lose some of them for sure." Mr. Nicely agreed and turned the bus toward the exit where there was a via-duct. The nose of the bus entered the tunnel when suddenly Mr. Nicely slammed on the brakes. He said, "Barbara, I don't think the bus will fit through the tunnel." He got out of the bus, took his cap off, and was scratching his head while looking at the clearance. I knew right away there was no way this bus was going through that tunnel. Now at this time we are parked in four lanes of traffic. Several people had already started to yell at us. I knew we didn't have much time. One of my students, who looked twenty-one, was hanging out the window picking up boys. I had to keep yelling out the bus door that she was too young and to move on. At the same time, a lady in a tank top with the phrase "kiss my redneck ass" screamed at me to let the air out of the tires. I said, "I appreciate your input, but are you crazy?" People were now screaming and honking at us while I said to the students, "This is a great example of when people don't know how to be patient. Too bad they didn't learn the Lifeline of Patience like you have learned."

We couldn't go forward and we couldn't go backwards. The other fourth-grade teacher, Mrs. Bogan, had on a bright red dress and her playground whistle around her neck. She said, "Barbara, you watch the kids and I'll take care of the traffic." She marched off the bus, started blowing her whistle, waving her arms, and yelling "back, back, back" to the four lanes of traffic.

A man came up to her and yelled, "Lady, who the hell do you think you are?"

Karen said, "I'm the fourth-grade teacher on that bus and we aren't going anywhere until this traffic backs up." The guy immediately jumped in and started directing the cars to back up. It was like the parting of the Red Sea. Mr. Nicely turned the bus around and headed for the entry.

At this point, it was well into the afternoon and we were starving. In this particular school district, it was a sin to consider eating and drinking on the bus. In the past, I had seen students nearly suspended for chewing gum. When I asked Mr. Nicely, who mind you was shaking and sweating profusely, if we could have the kids eat their lunch, he said he didn't care what I did. Needless to say, we all ate our packed lunches.

It is now late afternoon and we finally made it out of the speedway. As we approached the school, the students broke into song, singing, "That's What Friends Are For." It was so touching. You would have thought after being on a bus for nearly ten hours, without getting out of your seat and without a restroom break mind you, the kids would have been at each other's throats. They were wonderful, smiling and enjoying the time together. If there ever was a lesson on patience, this was it. Even to this day, I can't believe someone didn't ask to go to the bathroom while we were on the bus. Thank you, God.

The rest of the story: Mr. Nicely retired after this trip.

Final Word

Patience teaches us to be willing to wait for God's timing. We have learned to wait on God because He has his own timing for our lives.

"Wait for the Lord, be strong and take heart
and wait for the Lord."
Psalm 27

When I have been practicing patience, sometimes other lessons emerge:

Sometimes what you want now is not the right timing.

Sometimes what you want now isn't what you need.

Sometimes, in the time you are waiting for something to happen, you are actually preparing yourselves mentally and physically to accept a change.

Patience teaches us you can get through any situation. My second grandson has taught us so many lessons about patience. He was focused on basketball until he hurt his back. What would he do? He found a new and better path on the track team. Using patience and hope, he is always ready for the next event in his life. He never lets a disappointment turn into a discouragement.

Waiting isn't a bad thing and may be taking you to a better place than you thought. You never want to be waiting for the wrong bus. Know what you need to do, where you want to go, and if you need to develop new skills to get there.

If you every questioned the importance of patience. It takes time for the seasons to change, it takes time for the frog to emerge from the tadpole. Nature teaches patience.

"Adopt the pace of nature: her secret is patience."
Ralph Waldo Emerson

Affirmations for Patience

- Today I will be patient with others.

- Today I will be patient with myself.

- I am patient with a good attitude in everything I do today.

- I will wait on the Lord to guide me.

LESSON FIVE

Forgiveness

"It's one of the greatest gifts you can give yourself,
to forgive. Forgive everybody."
Maya Angelou

What is Forgiveness?

Forgiveness is recognizing a conflict and letting go of the past. When you release the resentment from a bad experience or the power of what another person had over you, you will be free to experience joy. Ask yourself these questions to identify the source of your unhappiness and see if forgiveness might help you.

Why are you feeling the way you do?

Has someone or something made you feel badly?

Is the source of your unhappiness you?

Forgiveness is not condoning whatever happened. Forgiveness is not for the other person as much as it is for you. If you had your joy stolen ask yourself:

Do I need to ask someone for forgiveness?

Do I need to forgive someone else?

Do I need to forgive myself and move forward?

When you have resentment toward another person, you can get a feeling of nervousness, anxiety or sadness. However, you can feel your body and mind change when you decide to seek a more positive emotion toward yourself or another person.

Forgiveness doesn't seem like that big a deal, but it is hard for some people to forgive others. When you have an unpleasant feeling toward someone, make up your mind you don't need to stay stuck in your emotions. Once you change your thinking, it doesn't take long to realize that simply forgiving another person or forgiving yourself will provide a sense of relief. After you decide to forgive and move forward, a fog lifts, and you will experience more joy. That is why forgiveness made the joy list.

"To forgive is to set a prisoner free, and to
realize that the prisoner was you."
Lewis B. Smedes

Guilty or Not Guilty

When you realize that you are losing your joy, you need to ask your-self "Am I guilty or not guilty?" If you are guilty, then try to make amends, because forgiveness works like magic to restore your soul. Asking a person to forgive you is the first step in regaining your joy when you feel guilty about something you may have done or said to another person.

If you are not guilty, then get over it and move ahead, instead of car-rying bad feelings. Dwelling too long in discontent reminds you that it is time to forgive yourself or someone else.

A big part of figuring out who to forgive is to seek to understand why you are feeling the way you do. Once when I was teaching fifth grade, a student named Billy told another student named Joe that he forgave him for spreading negative comments about him. Much to Billy's surprise when he told Joe he forgave him for what he had done, Joe had no idea what he was talking about. He actually hadn't spread negative thoughts about Billy. This example demonstrates that your mind can mess with you and make you feel a certain way, even when it isn't true. If a situation bothers you, be sure it just isn't a mistaken perspective on your part. In the act of forgive-ness, many times the truth will come out. In John 8:32 Jesus said, "You shall know the truth and the truth will set you free." I do believe this to be true.

Judgment and Mercy

In your life, there will be times when you will judge and be judged by others. At times, these judgements might be hurtful or misinformed. During these times, you need to consider using forgiveness. Forgiveness doesn't mean you are condoning actions. Forgiveness brings you peace of mind and releases your anger. When you can't forgive you carry a weight. Forgiving someone is a form of mercy. It is always better to show mercy instead of judgment. Be merciful.

"Judge not, and you will not be judged;
condemn not and you will not be condemned;
forgive, and you will be forgiven."
Luke 6:37

How Can You Apply Forgiveness in Your Life?

1. You can try to forget about what is bothering you; however, that usually doesn't work because memories that bother you have a way of sticking around.

2. You can do something to hurt the person who hurt you. However, this never works because that option keeps the problem going around like a merry–go-round and makes the situation worse.

3. If you have had an uneasy feeling for a long time, you need to start with forgiving yourself and realizing that your own thinking has been stealing your joy. You learn either to never make that mistake again or to forgive yourself for not thinking through a better decision. You can talk to yourself or write a message to yourself asking forgiveness.

4. You may realize that it is time to forgive others. The best is always face-to-face, but if they aren't around, texting, e-mailing, or a thoughtfully written apology also works. Keeping yourself locked in discontent is not good, and in many situations the other person may not realize that anything they did or said bothered you.

5. You cannot have true joy if you are holding on to unforgiveness. Resentment is one of life's greatest energy drainers but forgiving another takes the stress out of your life and

brings in contentment. Be sure your judgment isn't holding you back. Instead show mercy and forgive others. Once you have experienced the change, you will have control over your emotions, and you are on the path towards peace and joy.

Attitudes and Change

The words from Viktor E. Frankl, a Holocaust survivor during World War II, help us understand the power of attitudes and change.

> *"Everything can be taken from a man but one thing:*
> *the last of human freedoms to choose one's attitude in any*
> *given set of circumstances, to choose one's own way.*
> *When we are no longer able to change a situation, we are*
> *challenged to change ourselves."*
> Viktor E. Frankl

Just think of people like Mr. Frankl, who survived a Nazi prison camp or the people who survived the 1994 genocide in Rwanda where a million people were killed because of hatred. The Rwandans once again are trying to live side by side in peace, but that wouldn't be possible without a reconciliation process and the power of forgiveness. My oldest son witnessed the power of these processes when he traveled to Rwanda. We can learn from people who have practiced forgiveness in the direst circumstances.

Final Word

I can think of many times in life when I wish I had reacted differently to a situation. One time a very good friend of mine had disappointed me. I knew she had lied to me and instead of moving past the situation I stayed in my disappointment, sadness, and madness. Once I realized that my joy was connected to how I felt, not what my friend had done, I was able to move forward. I forgave myself for staying discontented longer than I needed to.

Once you decide you don't want to live with resentment about a person or situation, you can find instant relief with forgiveness and suddenly feel better. Forgiveness is a peace finder. Remember, the power is in your mind. Start forgiving today, no matter how small or large the problem is. Set yourself free.

> *"Be kind to one another, tender-hearted, forgiving each other,*
> *just as God in Christ also has forgiven you."*
> Ephesians 4:32

Affirmations for Forgiveness

- I will be tolerant of others and willing to forgive.

- I will be flexible when changes happen in my life.

- I will be patient with myself and others.

- I will be kind and compassionate towards others.

- I will be responsible for my actions and behavior.

- I will be a person who gives mercy, not judgment.

LESSON SIX
<u>Empathy</u>

*"I've learned that people will forget what you said,
people will forget what you did, but people will never
forget how you made them feel."*
Maya Angelou

What is Empathy?

Empathy is the ability to understand and share the feelings of others. How could having empathy help you find joy? When you use empathy, you actually sense what someone else is feeling and it guides how you respond. Empathy is different from sympathy, which is a shared feeling, usually of sorrow, pity or compassion for another person. With empathy, you put yourself in another person's shoes, often feeling things more deeply than if you just experienced sympathy.

From my experience, we are happier when we can be of service to others. When we use empathy, we are truly seeking to understand others and can be more compassionate. Empathy becomes a joy finder when we can respond to them with what they need.

> *"Be happy with those who are happy,*
> *and weep with those who weep."*
> Romans 12:15

How Can You Show Empathy?

1. Listen. When you listen to others, you are showing that you care and are interested in what others have to tell you. Listening to someone gives you insights into what he or she thinks or believes. Put yourself in the listener's shoes.

    There are five steps in being a good active listener:

    a. Your eyes: Use eye contact.

    b. Your ears: Listen to them. Hear what they are saying.

      c.   Your heart: Seek to understand and be empathetic.

      d.   Your undivided attention: Focus and pay attention without distraction.

      e.   You: Use your body and mind to focus and gain meaning of the conversation.

2. You are listening if you can talk about what was just said. Sharing a similar problem you have had sometimes helps. It isn't that you have all the answers, but that you care.

3. Show you care

      a.   Hug

      b.   High Five

      c.   Handshake

      d.   Be mindful of the situation around you. Be in the moment. When you are engaged in a conversation with someone, you don't notice anything else that is happening. Be there for others.

4. Love yourself so you can love others. You have to fill the lake before you irrigate the field.

5. Try not to be judgmental towards someone. Seek to understand before you conclude about his or her actions. Now this is stating the obvious, but if a person is being obnoxious or physical, of course ask him or her to stop or

go get help. Sometimes speaking up is an act of compassion instead of letting someone be a bully.

6. Do something kind without expecting anything back. Hold the door for someone or take food to a family who is going through an illness or a death. Thinking of the needs of another can be a demonstration of empathy.

7. Communication

a. Watch your tone of voice. Do you sound friendly?

b. Body language: Are your actions showing inclusion or are you shutting someone down? For example, to some people, crossing your arms in front of you can be a gesture that distances others.

c. Smile

"First of all, if you learn a simple trick, Scout, you'll get along a lot better with all kinds of folks. You never really understand a person until you consider things from his point of view . . . until you climb into his skin and walk around in it."
Harper Lee from *"To Kill a Mockingbird."*

Empathy in Education and Beyond

Empathy is needed in all professions, but especially in education. Teachers have empathy but sometimes students don't know it. Students need to know that their teachers truly care about how successful they are in school. Here are four interesting stories that made me realize the power of empathy in education.

Detention

I always liked to include students in the decision-making process when trying to improve school policy. One year I decided to visit middle school and high school detention rooms. My question to students in detention was: What would have prevented you from being sent to detention? The number one answer was, "I wish my teachers cared about me."

Ramon

I have had the opportunity in my life to meet many outstanding teachers. Most teachers sincerely care about their students, but some don't communicate that clearly by their actions or comments. For example, I was on my way into a bakery when I saw a boy sitting on the sidewalk, leaning against the building. He had a hoodie pulled over his head and was looking at a textbook. I said," Hi," and asked him where he went to school. He said he attended the middle school nearby, but he didn't need to go to first period. I had a sense that he was mad or sad about something. I asked him how things were going in school, and he replied, "Terrible."

I told him that I was a teacher. I could see he was unhappy and was there something he needed help with. He replied, "School would be nice if I had a teacher who cared."

I told him, "I am sorry about your situation. It is important to not let yourself get discouraged and instead take control of your learning. Get the information you need to help you, focus on doing your best, and keep a positive attitude about learning." He thanked me and I went into the bakery. When I came out, I gave him a sack of donuts. He said, "Thanks and you know you are the first person who ever asked me how school was."

To all students, teachers don't make you successful, you do, so do all you can to get along with teachers. We all make mistakes and might think someone doesn't care, but the truth is that some people don't know how to show they care. Misunderstandings happen when a teacher doesn't think a student cares, or a student doesn't think a teacher cares. We may not know exactly what someone is going through, but when we use empathy, we can sense when someone needs a smile or even a donut.

Rachael

I was in the bathroom of a school I was visiting. You can gain great insights about the climate of a school by listening to students talk in the restroom. A young girl named Rachael was in the bathroom and she said, "Hello," while I was washing my hands. I asked her how her day was going. She replied, "They want to medicate me because they think I'm wild." I told Rachael that I was here to visit her school and hoped I would see her again. I wished her luck. There obviously was a side of her I didn't see in the bathroom, and her teacher's perception of her being wild was on Rachael's mind.

After getting a feel of the school, I stopped in a third-grade classroom to observe the teaching. The students were sitting in a circle, and three of them had little sacks on their laps that contained three items that were important to them. They were taking turns sharing them with the class. Lo and behold, there was Rachael sitting in the circle, and we smiled at each other.

The first student started sharing the contents of his sack, which revealed a butterfly, a picture of his family, and a picture of his dog. He carefully pulled out the butterfly first. Much to my surprise, the teacher exclaimed, "Oh no, not another insect. We don't talk about those until spring." It was September and considering the high interest in insects, I was surprised the teacher would limit the topic to only one season.

After sharing the contents of the sack, each student could ask two other students if they had any questions or comments. During all this time, I noticed Rachael was sitting quietly and not causing any trouble. I would have expected more from a "wild" girl.

A boy named Rick then pulled out two baseball cards and a large dead grasshopper from his sack. The students let out a sigh when they saw the grasshopper. Just before the teacher could say a word, Rick quickly put the grasshopper back into his sack and began talking about his love for baseball and his favorite teams, the Chicago Cubs and the New York Yankees. When it was time for Rick to choose someone for a comment, Rachael said, "Ask Tommy, Ask Tommy."

The teacher immediately yelled at Rachael to leave the room and go to the hall. I followed shortly and stopped to talk with Rachael. My question was, "Why did you say, Ask Tommy?" Rachael said she knew she shouldn't say anything unless she was called on, but Tommy knew more about baseball than most adults. Some teachers might call that insightful or caring instead of wild.

I told Rachael that some teachers have tighter rules than others, and it was important that she tried to follow her teacher's procedures so she didn't get in trouble. She was smart enough and old enough to understand that. Rachael's last comment to me was, "Thanks for listening and for not thinking I'm wild." We hugged. I never saw Rachael again, but I have thought about her many times.

When we seek to understand, we usually see what is true. I wish the best for all the students in that third-grade class that loved insects, especially Rachael. Now that I think about it, maybe the teacher was having a bad day and just needed some empathy.

Boy on the Elevator

I was at a teacher's conference in a large hotel, when I met a young man on the elevator. He thought I was with the Mary Kay Conference, which I found hilarious. I told him I was a teacher and asked him, "Where do you go to school?" He replied that he had dropped out of school because no one cared whether he was in school or not. I said to him, "You have to care enough about yourself. You don't need other's caring to do well in school."

This was a turning point for me in how we help our students. Students need to care about learning themselves. I began communicating to teachers and parents to seek the power of empathy. Perhaps modeling empathy would show students that people care. Could helping students be successful be that easy? Did students need to understand that teachers wanted them to do well? Of course, students are responsible for their own success, but after all these situations, I couldn't help but think that empathy from teachers plays an important part in molding a successful student. I had a great insight from these four experiences. Perhaps modeling empathy would have an impact on how students felt about learning and other people. This concept applies not only to school but to all contexts of life.

Gary Phillips

While I was writing this lesson about empathy in education, great people in my life came to mind. Gary Phillips was one of those people. The last time I saw him was in Kansas City where we were both presenting. Gary was an educator and everything he said about education was what I believed and was trying to do. That is how my life has been. Amazing people have come into my life, validating my idea that perhaps education could change, and all students could find success as long as teachers understood how the brain learns and had empathy along the way.

Gary said one time, "If the horse is dead, it is time to dismount." In the eighties and nineties in education, it was time to get a new horse. Gary made me think if enough educators could see students as whom they could become, not just what they can remember, perhaps more students would embrace learning.

In tribute to Gary Phillips, here are some of his words of wisdom:

1. Don't try to become a better teacher than you are a person. Instead, strive to become a better person.

2. You get from students what you model to students. Don't complain about student apathy and disrespect; embellish enthusiasm and respect.

3. Teachers who believe some kids won't learn no matter what you do are correct.

4. Honor imagination as much as memory.

5. Use your professional x-ray to find gifts in students that others miss. Use your gathering of gifts to become a dream maker for students. You can't teach a student who doesn't have a dream.

6. The best teachers are also learners.

Thanks, Gary, for influencing many educators who dismounted the horse and found new direction.

Empathy is Contagious

I walked into a school that I was coaching and stopped at the principal's office to check in. There was a boy sitting in a chair and since the secretary was busy, I struck up a conversation with him. I asked, "What are you waiting for?" and he replied that he had to see the principal for talking out in class. I told him that was too bad but some teachers just couldn't stand that. Maybe he could try to wait to talk next time. He said he would try. I went into the office to visit with the principal. When I came out of the office I headed for the stairs and I heard the boy yell out, "Hey lady you forgot your bag." I couldn't believe it.

I told him that I had to go the third floor and if I had gone all the way up there and realized I had forgotten my bag, I would have had to come all the way back for it. I couldn't thank him enough. I hugged him and told him he was using empathy when he thought of how sad I'd be when I realized I had forgotten my bag.

The next morning, I came into the school and there was a classroom of students sitting against the wall waiting for everyone in their class to come out of the restroom. I thought to myself that there had to be a better way to do this. The students could have been writing something on clip-boards or at least the teacher could have been talking to the students about something. Heaven forbid they could have been trusted to return to the classroom and there could be a checker if anyone was missing.

Anyway, I said, "Good morning, my you are all being so patient waiting for the other boys and girls to come out of the restroom." A girl yelled out while pointing to a boy, "Robert is always in trouble. He never does anything right." When I looked at the boy named Robert, I realized it was the same boy who helped me the day before. I quickly replied," No, Robert is a wonderful boy, and he is so responsible. Hi Robert, it is so good to see you. Thanks again for helping me yesterday. I hope you have a great day." I gave him a little hug and he looked up and whispered, "Thanks for the empathy." I went up to the third floor with tears in my eyes.

I just want teachers to remember to seek to understand their students. When we try to see through our students' eyes and walk in their shoes, sometimes we can better understand why they do what they do. I am not condoning bad behavior but many times a little empathy will bring peace.

> *"Empathy: Could a greater miracle take place than*
> *for us to look through each other's eyes for an instant?"*
> Henry David Thoreau

Final Word

If you are on a path to find joy, empathy can help. Anytime you are seeking to understand someone else, you give joy to that person. Every day you need to do something that helps another person. It can be a smile or letting someone go ahead of you in a line or in traffic. Empathy is knowing the feelings of others. You see through other people's eyes and understand what they are going through. Caring is what you do because of empathy.

Affirmations for Empathy

- I can see through the eyes of others.

- I can feel through the hearts of others.

- I will seek to understand other people today.

- I can feel empathy for everyone I meet who needs it.

LESSON SEVEN

<u>Hope</u>

*"Hope is being able to see that there is
light despite all of the darkness."*
Desmond Tutu

What is Hope?

Hope is a feeling or expectation about something you want to have happen in your future. It makes you feel alive because you start thinking about possibilities. Hope is something that brings you the gift of joy from God. Hope leads into prayer. We may not get exactly what we are hoping for but thinking about it gets us up to start doing what is needed to make it happen.

My father's favorite song was "Look for the Silver Lining" by Chet Baker.

"Look for the silver lining
When ere a cloud appears in the blue
Remember, somewhere the sun is shining
And so the right thing to do is make it shine for you.
A heart, full of joy and gladness
Will always banish sadness and strife
So always look for the silver lining
And try to find the sunny side of life."

He was truly a remarkable person and always was thinking of new things to hope for in life. He was a painting contractor and every year he would dedicate a portion of his time painting houses for people who couldn't afford to have them painted themselves. One of the best lessons he taught me was at an amusement park called Riverside. We were in line for the rollercoaster behind an African American boy and his father. When it was their turn, the man taking tickets told them they didn't allow people like them to ride. My father was furious and told the ticket man if they couldn't ride, we won't ride. He told me in the car that he hoped I would see the day that all races would be included and accepted everywhere.

I kept his hope alive through my work. When President Obama was sworn in as our forty-fourth President of the United States, I was with a group of young African American boys. We were at the children's museum.

When I realized he was being inaugurated at that time, I asked if we could please watch the inauguration on television. The museum personnel walked us into a room to watch the ceremony. There wasn't a dry eye in the room. I realized the hope that this gave to everyone watching. It is possible to become anything you want. You need hope and action. That is what hope is.

> *"They say a person needs just three things to be truly*
> *happy in this world: Someone to love, something*
> *to do, and something to hope for."*
> Tom Bodett

Hold onto Your Hope

Paying attention to how you react to disappointments when your hopes are not met is an important lesson about staying on your joy journey. You need to hold onto your joy while you are going through disappointments. How you react is critical to your state of mind and your attitude during challenging times.

Many years ago, I thought a change would be good, so I sent in a teaching application to a neighboring district for a third-grade position. It never occurred to me that I wouldn't get the job because I had never interviewed for any previous job since positions had always been available for me. Why would I think this would be different? As a matter of fact, I was thinking how lucky they were to get me. I find that arrogance funny now that I look back. Not only did I not get the job, but I also didn't even get an interview. It was hard to believe.

If that wasn't disappointing enough, I also applied at that same time to another neighboring district and was thrilled that they granted me an interview. After leaving the principal's office when my interview was over, I stopped by the front desk and saw my rejection letter lying there where I couldn't have missed it. It was almost like I was supposed to see that I had been turned down for the job even before my interview.

Needless to say, rejection knocked my hopes down, and was a blow to my ego and confidence. When the new school year started, I was back in my classroom, happy to have my old job, when I received an unexpected notification that I had been named the Christa McAuliffe Teacher of the Year for Indiana. That allowed me to take a one-year sabbatical and design curriculum that would eventually be called C.L.A.S.S.

None of that would have happened if I had gotten either of the other jobs I applied and hoped for. We need to keep our joy in the storm and trust that God has a plan for our lives. His plan is much better than our plan, and His timing is usually different than ours. He knows what we are going through. We just have to remember to hold onto hope because there are better things ahead. What we think we need or want may not be true at all.

Lessons for me during this experience were to let go of my ego and know that as good as I was, I could always get better. I never forgot that I was blessed to be able to serve children and teachers. This experience started with hope for the wrong thing but ended with an educational journey that changed my life.

"What seems to us as bitter trials are often blessings in disguise."
Oscar Wilde

Realize that there is always hope with disappointment. The situation may turn out to be better than you think if you just hang on. When we have a disappointment, we need to examine the situation. Whatever your disappointment is, consider learning something new or changing parts of your life to help solve your problem. Ask yourself, what would be the best solution? Your reaction to your disappointment may be interfering with a better vision.

Accept what is making you mad or sad. The disappointment may be taking you to where you need to be. Have hope during your trials because there is light even after the darkest night. A lesson is around every corner; don't miss it. There are many steps on the journey to find joy and a disappointment may be one step. Keep your vision, let go of disappointment and hold on to hope.

"All great things are simple, and many can be expressed in a single word: freedom, justice, honor, duty, mercy, and hope."
Winston Churchill

Don't Let Anything Steal Your Joy

I had a habit of taking a bottle of Joy dish soap to teachers when I visited classrooms with the suggestion that if anyone was losing their joy, they could wash their hands with soap from the Joy bottle. You can always put a little joy in your life. Students and adults were reminded to not let anything steal their joy.

One day I was leaving a school and a student ran after me carrying a Joy bottle wrapped in brown paper towels. He said, "Mrs. Pedersen, why don't you send this to President Bush. I think he must be losing his joy with all the problems going on in the Middle East." Out of the mouths of babes, you will find great insights. Sometimes children have more empathy than we give them credit for, and it seems easy for them to believe in the power of hope. Perhaps if we trust them, they will lead us to a better world.

"Learn from yesterday, live for today, and hope for tomorrow.
The important thing is not to stop questioning."
Albert Einstein

Keep Life Simple

Keep life simple. Life doesn't need to be complicated all the time. Even a simple get together with friends can get out of control. It was Friday and I thought how fun it would be to have friends over for hamburgers, baked beans, and chips. The more I thought about who should come, my list of guests grew until I had the entire neighborhood coming. Then it occurred to me that I better rethink my menu. Hamburgers and beans turned into steaks, twice-baked potatoes, fresh green beans, rolls, and baked Alaska. Then, I began to panic because the house was a mess; and the empty flowerpots that had weeds growing out of them needed fresh soil and flowers. Oh, and I better get more porch furniture for everyone to be able to sit together and before I knew it, I had created a monster. The party would start in only a few hours, my husband was golfing, the kids were gone, and I was ready to ditch this crazy idea. What was I thinking of in the first place? If I had kept it simple and stayed with my original plan, I would still be excited, and the smaller group could have had great conversation. Keep it simple and life will be more fun. Why complicate everything? What more could you hope for than good friends or family enjoying a conversation?

Final Word

Pay attention to your strengths. You may be better prepared to move ahead with what could be possible in your life than you ever imagined. What are you hoping for? God may be working in your life right now to help you be aware and to help you follow the plan He has for your life. You have something of value to give. Trust His guidance.

"For I know the plans I have for you, declares the Lord,
plans to prosper you, and not harm you, plans to give
you HOPE and a future."
Jeremiah 29:11

Affirmation for Hope

- Please God guide me in the direction you would have me go. I want whatever you hope for me.

LESSON EIGHT
Learning

"Live as if you were going to die tomorrow.
Learn as if you were going to live forever."
Mahatma Gandhi

Learning

To live life to the fullest you never want to stop learning. Learning new things can happen many ways. You can learn from reading a book, talking to others, using technologies, and most of all through experiences. Every time you stretch your thinking to a new level, you are learning. Some of the greatest learning can be by accident. It just happens while you're waiting for something, watching an event, or at that moment when you say, "Ah ha."

The Learner Was Me

I had pitched my dittos and worksheets and was ready for a great year teaching second grade. My neat rows of desks were gone and were replaced with tables we called learning clubs. Since school had just started, I decided to have each learning club take a different element in the school and design a school of the future. We had the music room, the café, the math center, the reading center, and the playground. Each student had to write a narrative and include the math they used to construct their three-dimensional model. The custodian brought in five long tables for the students to use to build their future school. Friday everyone was to present their project.

Friday came and the students were so excited to share! As the students presented, I was sitting in the back of the room and I couldn't believe the level of thinking these children were using. I had never given students in past years the opportunity before to show work through their interest and creativity. In the past, my students had been too busy doing unrelated worksheets about isolated skills. They weren't allowed to do creative work until they completed their worksheets (and that never happened).

The lunchroom group designed a way to eliminate lines in the cafeteria by creating a refrigerated glass wall where you could see and select the meal that you wanted. Some of the food was grown in the school garden where each grade level had a section to maintain.

The music room group came up with pictures of instruments that you could tap to create different instrumental sounds to go with the music they were singing. They could compose music using keyboards embedded in their desks. This was before computers, which made all their ideas seem even more amazing and the fact this school served low economic students who had not had a lot of experiences.

The last group was the playground group. Bud was the team leader. Now, Bud was on the "Oh, no! I have him in my classroom" list. His first-grade teacher even sent me a note at the beginning of the year saying, "he had nothing between his ears." What happened next was the beginning to an amazing year for Bud that turned his academic life around. Picture this: A long table covered with green paper and a large blue lake in the middle. The students then took blue paper and made a waterfall covered with glitter from the lake on the table to the floor. Under the table there were different underwater creatures hanging by strings. At the side of the lake there was a dock with boats made from three long, yellow, plastic dishes like the ones they used at Dairy Queen for banana splits. There was a large Styrofoam boat with saran wrap over the bottom that resembled a glass-bottomed boat.

Bud got up and explained that students could go out on the lake and ride on the big glass bottomed boat to discover underwater life. Another choice was to get in the yellow boats and go over the waterfall. It was actually the waterfall of wisdom. You were "dumb" when you started your boat ride. After you rode over the waterfall of wisdom you became very smart (his words exactly). There was a ladder of tongue depressors and yarn leading back up to the top of the table from the floor. After I asked what this was for, he said, "When you go over the Waterfall of Wisdom you will be lower than the playground. You will need to take this hydraulic lift up to the top of the lake so you can enter the school." Bud had plenty of knowledge and wisdom between his ears. He hadn't had the opportunity to use his brain. I never went back to rows of desks and dittos. I learned that learning happens when the lesson comes alive.

The Two Steps of Learning

1. What do you understand?

2. What can you do with what you understand?

Understanding the elements of something is the first step of learning. In golf, I may learn and understand what a driver, a putter, an iron, a tee, a putting green and a flag are, but it doesn't mean I know how to play the game of golf. If I want to get to the second step of learning, I need to understand how to use those elements in my life. If I want to play the game of golf, I may need to take lessons or go golfing with someone who knows how to play the game. I need to know how to swing the clubs and how to hit the ball in certain situations. This will require practice. It also requires feedback, right away, so I am not practicing incorrect techniques that could turn into bad habits. All of this will take time, support, patience, and effort.

"It's not that I'm so smart, it's just that
I stay with problems longer."
Albert Einstein

Meaningful Information is Easier to Learn

The more we understand the world around us, the more connections we can make. When connections happen, the world around you has more meaning. It is very hard to learn or understand something that doesn't make sense to you.

For example, I was watching a riverboat called the Mark Twain on the Ohio River. It had a sign on deck for the Becky Thatcher Diner. I could sit and watch the majestic boat on the river but knowing who Mark Twain and Becky Thatcher were made more connections for me and gave me more meaning. Does everyone need to know that? Of course not, but the more you know, the more you understand. I imagine that there were people watching the same boat who thought Mark Twain was just the name of the man who ran the boat, and Becky Thatcher was the name of the cook for the diner.

Now if you apply what you know, you will be surprised at how much more you can understand. It is like the rest of the story. I don't know how to drive a riverboat or run a diner. To be honest I don't ever want to do either, but lots of people like doing both of those things. Learning something takes interest first. No matter what your age is, give yourself adventures every week to broaden your thinking and to find new things you can be passionate about. Helen Keller once said, "Life is either a daring adventure or nothing at all." Just imagine what you can accomplish in life if you keep learning.

Keep Thinking

One time I was in a schoolboard meeting and I was asked to discuss best practices in education connected to what we know about the brain and learning. In attendance was the school board, the principals of the school district I coached, teachers, and parents. One parent was criticizing my ideas and thoughts about what education should be today. After a couple of hours, I thought this was never going to end and I said, "We are just trying to teach your children how to think." She replied, "I don't want my children to think." I couldn't believe it. The head of the board meeting said," This meeting is over." I never forgot this and never lost my passion in teaching students how to think. This was an experience I was very grateful for because it gave me courage to stand up for students.

"Education is not the learning of facts but
the training of the mind to think."
Albert Einstein

Learning about Character

As we go through life, we are given different trials about how to act in different situations. The Life Goals give us a framework for learning about character.

THE LIFE GOALS

Do the right thing.

Treat people right.

(Even if you don't feel like it)

Just knowing the Life Goals doesn't make us a better person. We have to understand them in different situations and practice doing the right thing and treating people right in different situations. It is the practice and application that makes us a better person.

Knowing that we know how to act won't make us act better until we practice actually doing what is right in different situations. We can know a lot but if we don't put our knowledge into action, just knowing doesn't change us as a person. Once we take what we know and practice using that information to do something right, then we are learning. We need to assess and ask ourselves how we are improving from our practice. Saying the following pledge every day will help remind us of the right thing to do.

LIFE GOAL PLEDGE

I will treat people right even if I don't feel like it.

I will do the right thing even if I don't feel like it.

My will power is stronger than what I think or how I feel.

I am smarter than I think I am.

All things are possible.

Good news is coming my way.

To understand how to use the Life Goals: treat people right; and do the right thing, we use what is called the Lifelines (character traits) to help guide us. The Lifelines give us direction on what behaviors are appropriate for different situations in our lives. For example, if we have to wait in line for something or if traffic is bad, we could do the right thing and treat people right by using the Lifeline of patience. The Lifelines are the traits that build our character. Below is a list of Lifelines that will help guide you throughout life in meeting your Life Goals: treating people right and doing the right thing.

INTEGRITY: To act according to a sense of what is right and wrong

PATIENT: To wait without complaining

KIND: To be helpful to others; Doing something nice for others

HONESTY: To be truthful

INITIATIVE: To do something of one's own free will

FLEXIBILITY: To be willing to alter plans when necessary

PERSEVERANCE: To keep at it and not give up

ORGANIZATION: To plan, arrange, and keep things orderly and ready to use

SENSE OF HUMOR: To laugh and be playful without harming others

EFFORT: To do your best

COMMON SENSE: To use good judgment

PROBLEM SOLVING: To create solutions in difficult situations

RESPONSIBILITY: To respond when appropriate; To be accountable for your actions

FRIENDSHIP: To make and keep a friend through mutual trust and caring

CURIOSITY: A desire to investigate and seek understanding of one's world

COOPERATION: To work together toward a common goal or purpose

COURAGE: To act according to one's beliefs

RESOURCEFUL: The ability to respond to challenges and opportunities

RESPECT: To consider worthy

WELLNESS: To take care of your body and mind

MANNERS: To use social skills in different situations

JOYFUL: To share happiness with others

GRATEFUL: To be thankful

RESILIENT: To adjust easily to misfortune or change

GENEROSITY: To be giving and willing to share

SELF-CONTROL: Control exercised over one's self

TRUSTWORTHY: To be dependable and truthful

FORGIVE: To cease to feel resentment towards someone

FAIRNESS: Free from self- interest, partiality, prejudice, or favoritism

Developing Your Character Happens Throughout the Day

Experiences tend to confirm or change our thinking about something. I arrived early that morning to an impoverished inner-city school. I was going to coach fifth-grade teachers on student character development. The office was hectic because there were seven teachers out and no subs. I told the principal I would be happy to substitute teach instead of coach if that would help. She said I could pick any grade, so I chose first grade. How hard could that be? My first year of teaching I taught forty-seven first graders all year, so, one day with twenty-five students would be a piece of cake.

I ran upstairs to tell one of the fifth-grade teachers that I wouldn't be coaching her today. She was talking to someone, so I stopped at a table of students and said, "Good Morning, how are you today." One of the girls said, "What the hell, it isn't your business." I couldn't believe it and left to go to my first-grade class. I was thrilled I hadn't picked fifth.

The bell rang and I was at the door to greet my new students. After I greeted them, they started rolling around on the floor. In the first five minutes I heard every swear word I knew. I told everyone to take their seats and my name was Mrs. Pedersen. That prompted everyone to fall out of their chairs. I thought good grief this is a hot mess. I told them to join me in circle at the front of the room. They slid to the front, jumped on each other, and swore like sailors. I told them to go back to their seats. They skipped and ran all the way.

At this point, all I could wonder about was how in the world did this teacher teach. In her lesson plans, there was a picture of the most intricate helicopter I had ever seen on paper for the students to cut out. I started to pass them out and the first boy who got his said, "If you think I'm cutting this out, you're crazy." He was right. Who in the world could cut these tiny pieces out without surgical sheers? I quickly picked up the few I had distributed and at that moment a lady entered and yelled, "Shut up. Ritalin line up." The room got dead silent and about ten boys lined up while she unlocked two padlocks to get the bottle of Ritalin out of a cabinet. She started giving pills to the kids who were in line. I suggested that J.J. and Mike should be in the Ritalin line too, but sadly, they weren't on her list. I was thrilled with her control of the class and asked her if she would be with me long. Unfortunately, she said nothing except she would be back after lunch for second doses. As soon as she left, one of the boys told me there was an extra key for the Ritalin cabinet taped under the desk, if I wanted a pill for myself. I thanked him and told him I would consider doing that later.

I quickly noticed they had art at 9:00 so I told them they would have to miss art if they didn't settle down. I can still hear them yelling, "We hate art. We don't want to go to art." "Ok," I said. "You are going to have double art if you don't sit down." That got their attention. It was 8:45 and I felt I had been there for two days. We hiked up to the second floor to be greeted by the tallest art teacher I had ever seen yelling, "Get in there." I was prying the kids off the coat hooks and said, "You heard her."

I couldn't believe it. I ran downstairs and tore out the math sheets for them to do and put them on their desks with a pencil. I had to break pencils in half for them to each have one. I knew I would have to work fast when they came back. I ran upstairs and lo and behold they walked out of art like little soldiers. I don't know what she did to them, and I didn't care.

We got downstairs to our room and I noticed every single student had shredded their art picture. I didn't say a word about it. I held the wastebasket and I told them to drop their confetti in the trash can. They were to enter quietly and do the math that was on their desks. One boy thanked me for getting the math sheets ready, and another one reminded me that I would be in big trouble for breaking pencils. I replied that I didn't care because they all needed pencils.

As they worked on their math sheets, I quickly went from desk to desk asking their names and if they had any brothers or sisters. I knew that for this day to be a success, I needed to build a relationship with these kids. They needed to know that I cared and was there to support them. Going to each of them individually was the first step in building that kind of trust. Afterall, who was I? They thought I was just some substitute that would never come back.

The day wasn't perfect, but it was getting better. We created chart stories about themselves and decided we could hear each other if we talked one at a time. A mother came in to visit in the afternoon while the class was doing an activity with their crayons. Suddenly, some boys yelled out at the back table that she wasn't sharing. I replied, "Who's not sharing?" It was the visiting mother. I could go on, but I wanted you to get an idea about this day and how I looked at how important it was to build inclusion and develop positive relationships. Learning begins with a classroom that is absent of threat and has a trusting environment. Developing character is not in isolation, it happens throughout the day.

The announcement came over the loudspeaker that teachers could pick the good citizen of the day. I laughed out loud and said, "You have to be kidding. None of us were good citizens including me. By the way does anyone even know what a good citizen is?" One boy said, "No, but they get to go to the office and get a piece of candy."

The teachers next door came in after everyone left and said I was the third substitute this week and the other two had walked out before 10:00 a.m. I felt a little satisfaction hearing that but more than that, the day had changed my approach to teaching character. The students needed Life Goals. They needed behavior procedures. No one understood the expectations at the school. Students needed to build relationships. If you don't know how to get there and you don't know who your traveling with, you will never get to where you are going. So much needed to happen for learning to take place.

What Does Learning Take?

Learning anything in life will take:

- Interest: Do you want to learn something? Do you have resources to get the knowledge you need to understand the lesson?

- Meaning: Is what you are learning meaningful? It is hard to learn something that doesn't make sense.

- Collaboration/Assessment: Other people's input about how you are doing. You might practice doing something over and over and be practicing it incorrectly. We can get better with the collaboration and expertise of others. Constantly

assessing your progress and getting feedback from someone reminds you if you are improving.

- Relationships: If you are learning something with other
  people, it is important that you build a relationship with
  the others. Sharing your progress will be easier with others
  you can trust.

- Time: Can you put in the adequate time to learn what you
  want to do? Learning takes time. If you don't want to spend
  time on what you are learning, you won't be successful.

The Power of Meaning

I want to expand a moment on the importance of how powerful
meaning is in the learning process. I was observing a second-grade classroom. The teacher had the class doing a "short e" worksheet. Their task
was to write the "short e" words that matched the pictures on the page. As
the teacher circulated around the room, she began marking the incorrect
answers on the student's work. What became difficult to watch was her lack
of communication with the students in trying to understand their reason-
ing and rationale for their answers. She never took into consideration their
schema and to make things worse, never gave any feedback to the students.
She was too busy marking her red x's on their pages.

I positioned myself on the opposite side of the room from the teacher
and began talking with some of the students. One student in the front row,
J.J., had written the word "red" next to a picture of an elf. I told him that
was brilliant because that little guy in the picture wears red a lot. I asked
him if he knew the little people who helped Santa? He looked at me like I
was crazy. I said, "Have you ever heard of an elf?" He said, "An elf? No, I
have never heard of that. I wrote the word red because I have a red shirt on,
so I thought since he has a shirt on, it was probably red and red is a short
e sound." Then I told him that was a picture of an elf and it was a "short e"
sound. I agreed with him that red was a "short e" sound and his rationale

was good, but knowing your teacher, she probably wants to see elf; and you might want to write it quickly because she is getting close to you." He quickly wrote elf. It is very hard to teach "short e" words with pictures that have no meaning for the student. This is true of anything. Meaningful information and schema help us understand.

The next classroom I observed was next door and they were studying short vowel words in general. The teacher wrote a word on the board and asked the class to say it. The first word was "mat". She asked if anyone knew what that was and one boy said, "Yes, I know a boy named Matt." The teacher replied that, "This mat was a rug." She continued the lesson, writing words down on the board and getting the same type of answers. Students were relaying what they thought the word meant based on their prior experiences. Experience is the best way to create meaning. I stayed behind and suggested to the teacher that perhaps walking the class down to the front door of the school and showing them the "mat" and having them even wipe their feet on the "mat" would help create meaning for them. Words that don't have meaning are just letters on a page. Case closed.

Never too Late to Learn

After doing a teaching workshop, I needed to get to the airport. A group of nuns could take me, but I would need to go with them first to watch a play titled Mark Twain. It was going to be at a local outdoor theater. That sounded great to me. While we were watching the play I needed to go to the restroom. It was my first experience with a porta-potty. After using the restroom, I couldn't see how to turn on the water in the little sink. When I came out, I asked how you turned on the water; I had tried everything. Much to my shock that wasn't a sink. The little white bowl that I had touched all over was in fact a urinal. There was no running water. I sat through the rest of the play holding my hands in front of me. I figured the nuns just thought I was praying.

Final Word

Remember school is never out.

Affirmations for Learning

- I will look forward to learning something new today.

- I am passionate about _____.

- I will share something I learned today with someone.

LESSON NINE

<u>Gratitude</u>

*"Gratitude makes sense of our past, brings peace for today,
and creates a vision for tomorrow."*
Melody Beattie

We Have a Lot to be Thankful For

When I was deciding my path to take in life there were only three professions for women. You could be a nurse, a secretary, or a teacher. I hated vomit, so nursing was out! I knew at an early age that being a secretary was not for me. My high school teacher even commented how appalled she was about my typing skills and took me off the yearbook staff. This left education. As I have said earlier, trust God, for He knows the path and purpose of our lives. I am thankful that He directed me to being a teacher. It has been my passion and purpose throughout my life in serving others for over sixty years and counting. This brings me to gratitude. Being thankful in your life will bring you joy immediately. I am thankful every day for serving educators in helping our future generations succeed.

Regardless of who you are or what you do in life, every day is a day to practice gratitude. It may be that you are thankful for your car starting this morning or something greater like being thankful for your job, for your children, for the people in your life! Being grateful will help you appreciate your past and rejoice in today. To get you started, here is a list of things I want you to consider:

God

Family

Friends

Nature

Pets

Health

Learning

The Arts

Profession

Sports

Freedom

Life

Your Ideas

Your hopes

Your dreams

When Do You Need to Practice Gratitude?

Gratitude isn't the end; it is the beginning. Don't wait till something is over to express gratitude. Be grateful along the way. Be grateful to be free to choose any dream you want. Be grateful that you are free to follow your passion for anything, as long as you are willing to do what it takes to make it come true. Be grateful that you have an idea to pursue and the effort and perseverance to make it succeed.

An attitude of gratitude will bring you more joy than you ever imagined. It can help motivate you to put forth your personal best in pursuing your desires. There is nothing like a positive mental attitude. It can give you the courage to attempt anything.

> *"Enjoy and be thankful for the little things, for one day*
> *you may look back and realize they were the big things."*
> Robert Brault

How Can You Be Thankful when Disappointments Happen?

Some of the most important lessons I have learned in life have been from disappointing situations or mistakes that I made. How could you ever be grateful for a disappointment? One that comes to mind was when I was a junior at Butler University as a student teacher in a local elementary school. My mentor teacher had three different reading groups doing the exact same thing. I thought it seemed like a waste of instructional time since some of the students were outstanding and some needed extra assistance. Every Friday our student teaching class would meet at the university to talk about what we learned that week. When it was my turn, I said, "I think time could be used better for diverse instruction in reading groups." The professor stopped me cold and yelled, "Barbara, you don't have the right to think what should be happening in a classroom. You have no experience. Learn the lessons that I am teaching and don't even think about what you would do or wouldn't do if you were in that classroom." To be honest that affected me for a long time. I thought maybe I wasn't smart enough to know what the right things were to do in a classroom if they weren't explained in a textbook.

Fast forward two years. I was attending an educational conference in California. The instructor was showing us new ways to present information to students. She was outstanding and was talking my language. Suddenly she turned to the audience and pointed her finger towards me and said, "Don't ever think you aren't good enough to come up with new ideas to help students learn. We need teachers that can think." I felt that message was meant for me and I have been eternally grateful for it my whole life. It started me on a path of thinking and discovering the best instruction for meeting the needs of all students. When you are disappointed about something that happened to you, remember there may be the day that you are grateful it happened.

Thinking Revisited

For years, I would work with schools in building an environment that is conducive for learning and with teachers on how to make the learning process come alive for their students. I had been working with Rebecca, an outstanding teacher in southern Indiana, who learned to integrate music, art, movement, and firsthand experiences into every lesson she taught. It was life changing for her students. Talk about a meaningful education! This was it.

The following year, I was coaching in a district that was near Rebecca's school. I decided to stop and observe her magical instruction to give me a lift. A lot had changed in that district. Teachers were now required to prepare the students for the state test by following a scripted teacher's manual. All students in each grade level needed to be reading the same books at the same time. After hearing this news, I immediately felt sick to my stomach. Educators in this district had taken a giant step backwards in providing the education students deserved. I couldn't believe I was watching Rebecca teach with her scripted manual, knowing how capable she was as a creative educator. When the children went out for recess I said to her, "I am so sad you have stopped engaging students in learning." Rebecca replied, "I was sad too, seeing my students lose interest in school, but after I started instructing with everything scripted, I found this was an easy way to teach. I didn't have to stay after school or work on weekends. Everything I needed was in my teacher's manual. I like it now. I don't even have to think."

Where are we headed in education if students and teachers don't have to think?

Today's students will be the ones to take us to tomorrow's possibilities. All the new music, art, building designs, cures for illnesses, environmental improvements, inclusion for all people and many more ideas will never happen if today's students do not know how to think and make well informed decisions.

You may be asking yourself, Barbara, how could you possibly find gratitude in these disappointments? Disappointments will happen but I believe God is always with us and I don't need to be discouraged. I ask for the right path to travel and the courage to stand up for ideas that I truly believe are right for children and educators. I am eternally grateful for God's guidance and love during any trial that life hands me. It is times like these that have always motived me to stay the course in improving our educational system. Don't let disappointments get in your way of pursuing what is right. Be thankful, learn from the disappointment and move forward.

"The size of your success is measured by the strength of your desire;
the size of your dream; and how you handle
disappointment along the way."
Robert Klyosaki

Praying For a Better Day

One of the best ways I know to practice gratitude is through prayer. You can pray at any time, giving God thanks along the way. A prayer can be as simple as "Thank you God." Many times, I pray to God to reveal a spiritual lesson to me and ask Him if for guidance. The sky may not part or an angel may not appear, but if you are quiet and listen, sometimes an answer will reveal itself to you. Many times, I will wake up in the morning and have an epiphany about my prayer.

In life, I am always reminded that all situations are in God's hands. Remember that God loves you no matter what. That is something to be thankful for. He will try to encourage you in His way and change your concerns into gratitude.

Wait for the Lord; Be strong, and let your
heart take courage; wait for the Lord."
Psalms 27:14

Expectations When You Practice Gratitude

Gratitude is our last lesson for a good reason; you will never completely find joy without it. Furthermore, it incorporates all of our previous lessons. Gratitude can change your perspective about things and because of having gratitude, your mind may be persuaded to change. Gratitude is a choice to use every day and can encourage you to forgive or show empathy toward someone. Negative thoughts and experiences can be changed into positive ones in God's timing and that is when we learn real lessons about life.

If you want to feel better about yourself and feel healthier, be grateful for something. When we get rid of "stinking thinking" our mental health improves and life doesn't seem so complicated. When we look for the good in others instead of the bad, life takes on a new meaning. Why use gratitude every day? You will be a happier person who is content with life.

"There is always a message in everyone that has yet to be told.
You just have to remember your roots and know that
God's strength will guide you in ways you can't imagine."
Jack Pedersen

Joy Journal

I was at church one Sunday and the minister was talking about "Let There Be Joy." After the sermon, I started Joy Messages by writing what I was thankful for on my daily calendar. After a few weeks, I soon realized that I needed more room to write. My lists had overtaken the calendar and I was forced to use an actual book of blank pages which I entitled my 'Joy Journal". Since that sermon many years ago, I have faithfully used my Joy Journal as a way to practice gratitude.

I encourage you to start your own Joy Journal. Begin by simply writing or drawing about three things you are thankful for on a weekly basis. You don't need to be an amazing artist. Before I give you the wrong idea, my artwork includes stick people.

It is important to think about what you are thankful for because it will put things in perspective for you. You may be happier than you think you are. As you practice gratitude, you will recognize its importance in creating a positive state of mind and even positive actions. On days when there doesn't seem to be anything to be thankful for, look again. When we have gratitude, we find joy.

"As we express our gratitude, we must never forget that
the highest appreciation is not to utter words, but to live by them."
John F. Kennedy

Final Word

Congratulations! You now know the secret of making your journey through life a Joy Journey. We have a lot to be thankful for! Don't forget that especially when you are having a bad day. If you are not happy with the way your life is going, check to see if you are following your passion. Life is too short to be doing something you don't like. If you have trouble finding something to be thankful for then change your mind and look at all the amazing things around you. Pay attention to what you pay attention to. That will help you find gratitude. The best way to start and end your day is with a grateful heart. Be thankful that you are alive and that you know God. Be thankful for trees, sky and all the wonderful things in nature. That will bring you joy!

> *"It is a funny thing about life, once you begin to take note of the things you are grateful for, you begin to lose sight of the things that you lack."*
> Germany Kent

Affirmations for Gratitude

- I give God my gratitude today.

- I will appreciate others and not judge them.

- I will live in the moment today.

- Yesterday is history, tomorrow is a mystery, today is a gift. That is why we call it the present.

ACKNOWLEDGEMENTS

There are not enough pages in this book to name everyone I am thankful for, but my greatest thanks is to God. He will direct our steps to lead us into the future. May His love and guidance and understanding be a beacon for all of us.

Special thanks to the following people whose words and wisdom have made a difference in my life. I wouldn't have experienced the joy I have had without crossing their paths.

God

Jesus

Holy Spirit

Saint Paul the Apostle

Luke, the Evangelist

Gloria Laverty

Genni Pedersen

Katie Pedersen

Jimmy, Lindsey, and Lucy Sharp

Jim McMillan (My son from another mother)

Ruby Butler (My daughter from another mother)

Aaron Roberson

Cindy Mitchell

Jan Holsopple

Karen Geiger

Theresa Knipstein Meyer

Molly Dougherty

Martha Kaufeldt

Julie Lovell

Margaret Buchanan

Gino Johnson

The C.L.A.S.S. Staff (past, present, and future)

Walt Disney

Ginger Gramm

Rick Brown

Alan Cohen

Richard Bach

Ralph Waldo Emerson

Henry David Thoreau

Mitch Daniels Jr.

Randall L. Tobias and the Family Foundation

Suzanne "Susie" Hazelett

Dr. H. Dean Evans

Dr. David Hutton

Pat Wolfe

John Sloggett

Mike Pinto

Susan Kovalik

Yoda

Snoopy

A special thanks to my editor, Sally Tanselle. I knew what I wanted to say, but she showed me how to put my thoughts on the page. Her tireless effort made this book possible. More than once, I felt we were Thelma and Louise.

My dear friend, Rinkey Boleman, who took the extraordinary photographs that bring this book to life. Her eyes put the images to the lessons I am sharing. Thank you, Rinkey.

My dear High School friends and especially Marty Harding, Pat Dunbar, Jody Hollenback, Deanna Durrett, Sherry Brooks Herzer, Sandy Stava, Nancy Young, and Carole Woodruff

My college friends Peggy Scheper, Bonnie Garrett and Sandy Cheney

My amazing lifelong friends in the First Tuesday Group

My Beloved Book Club friends who have kept me on the journey

At the beginning of C.L.A.S.S. a special group of educators changed the way we think about teaching. A special thanks goes to the following educators:

Robin Lynch and the Central Elementary staff and Oak Trace Elementary staff

Susan Brash Heinz and the Amy Beverland staff

Beth Neidermeyer and the Fishback Creek Public Academy staff

Susan Howard and the Lowell Elementary staff

A wise friend once told me not to start thanking people in public because you will forget to mention someone. A special thanks goes out to you. You know who you are. Thank you.

You have learned in this book that joy is a journey, not a destination. I hope the lessons about life, character, love, and laughter helps you find joy along the path you have chosen to travel. Now, may the rest of your journey begin again with new eyes. Let Joy Be Your Journey!

To contact Barbara: Barbara@joyofclass.org